INTRODUCTION

Financial stress is one of the most common struggles people face in today's world. Whether it's worrying about making ends meet, managing debt, or dealing with unexpected expenses, money issues have a way of impacting every aspect of our lives. Financial stress doesn't just stay in your wallet—it seeps into your mind, your relationships, and even your physical well-being. It's no surprise that financial issues are consistently ranked as one of the top causes of anxiety and stress worldwide.

When financial stress becomes overwhelming, it can feel like there's no way out. The weight of unpaid bills, shrinking savings, or uncertainty about the future can create a cycle of worry, sleepless nights, and feelings of helplessness. But here's the good news: financial stress is something you can manage, and this book is here to help you take those first steps.

The goal of this guide is not to promise instant wealth or quick fixes, but to provide practical and useful strategies for reducing financial stress. Whether you're dealing with crushing debt, unexpected expenses, or just feeling overwhelmed by your current financial situation, the tools and techniques in this book are designed to help you regain control and reduce the anxiety that money troubles can bring.

We'll start by helping you understand exactly what financial stress is and how it affects you. Then, we'll dive into the practical steps you can take to organize your finances, reduce expenses, and build a foundation of financial resilience. You'll learn how to set realistic goals, handle debt without panic, and develop a plan for the future—no matter how much money you have right now.

Financial stress may be a part of life, but it doesn't have to control you. This book will show you how to take manageable steps towards financial clarity and peace of mind. Whether you're starting from scratch or just need to refine your financial habits, this guide is here to offer support, direction, and encouragement.

By the end of this book, you'll have a clearer picture of your financial situation, actionable steps to improve it, and the confidence to face your financial challenges head-on. The journey to financial stability is a personal one, but you don't have to face it alone. Let this book be your companion as you move toward a future with less stress and more financial peace.

CHAPTER 1: UNDERSTANDING FINANCIAL STRESS

What Causes Financial Stress?

Financial stress can stem from a variety of sources, often rooted in our daily experiences and responsibilities. One of the most common causes is debt. Whether it's student loans, credit card balances, or a mortgage, debt can feel like a constant weight hanging over your head. The obligation to make monthly payments, often with interest, can quickly escalate into overwhelming anxiety if you're struggling to keep up. The pressure of owing money, combined with the fear of falling behind or defaulting, creates a vicious cycle that many people find hard to break.

Income instability is another significant source of financial stress. Living paycheck to paycheck, dealing with unpredictable work schedules, or facing the threat of job loss can make it difficult to plan ahead or feel secure about the future. This lack of certainty around how much money will be coming in each month can lead to sleepless nights and constant worry about how to cover basic living expenses.

High living expenses further exacerbate financial stress. In today's world, the cost of housing, healthcare, and even groceries continues to rise, often outpacing wages. The stress of simply affording a place to live or covering the cost of essential needs can make it feel like you're always struggling to stay afloat, no matter how hard you work. The feeling of not being able to meet these expenses, despite putting in the effort, can be deeply demoralizing.

Unexpected costs also contribute to financial stress. Life is full of surprises, and unfortunately, many of them come with a price tag. Whether it's an unplanned medical bill, car repair, or emergency home maintenance, these sudden expenses can quickly throw your finances into disarray. If you don't have a financial cushion in place, an unexpected cost can push you further into debt or create panic about how you'll pay it off.

Ultimately, financial stress is often caused by a combination of these factors. When they pile up, they can create a sense of powerlessness and lead to emotional and physical strain. Understanding the root causes of your financial stress is the first step toward addressing it and finding relief. By identifying the specific factors causing your anxiety—whether it's debt, income instability, high living costs, or unexpected expenses—you can begin to take the necessary steps to regain control over your financial life.

How Financial Stress Affects Your Health

Financial stress doesn't just weigh heavily on your mind—it can take a toll on your overall health as well. The mental strain of constantly worrying about money can seep into every aspect of your well-being, impacting both your physical and emotional state. Over time, this stress can manifest in ways that disrupt your daily life, your relationships, and your ability to function optimally.

One of the most immediate effects of financial stress is the mental burden it creates. Anxiety is a common response, with persistent thoughts about debt, bills, and financial insecurity keeping you on edge. This anxiety can lead to overthinking, irritability, and a sense of helplessness, making it difficult to focus on anything else. You may find yourself constantly running worst-case scenarios through your mind, unable to relax or find peace. In extreme cases, financial anxiety can contribute to panic attacks or even lead to depression, especially if the stress feels never-ending.

Sleep is often one of the first things to suffer when you're under financial stress. Insomnia is a frequent consequence, as worries about money can keep your mind racing long after you've gone to bed. Lying awake at night, replaying your financial situation, can create a vicious cycle: the less sleep you get, the more stressed and irritable you become, which only worsens your ability to think clearly and make sound financial decisions. Over time, chronic sleep deprivation can affect your memory, concentration, and even your immune system, leaving you more vulnerable to illness.

Physically, financial stress can have serious consequences as well. Chronic stress has been shown to raise levels of cortisol, a hormone linked to the body's fight-or-flight response. Elevated cortisol levels over a prolonged period can lead to a range of health issues, including high blood pressure, headaches, and even heart disease. Stress can also trigger unhealthy coping mechanisms, such as overeating, smoking, or excessive drinking, as a way to temporarily escape or numb the anxiety. These behaviors not only compound the stress but also increase the risk of long-term health problems.

In addition to the mental and physical toll, financial stress can strain your relationships. Money is a common source of conflict in partnerships and families, with disagreements about spending, saving, or debt leading to arguments and tension. The constant worry about finances can make it difficult to be emotionally available to your loved ones, which may cause further distance or misunderstandings. This breakdown in communication can lead to feelings of isolation, as you may feel you can't turn to others for support.

Ultimately, financial stress affects your overall well-being in profound ways. It's not just about the numbers in your bank account—it's about the emotional and physical fallout that comes with it. Recognizing how stress is impacting your health is a crucial step toward managing it. By taking action to reduce the sources of financial stress in your life, you can begin to alleviate its damaging effects on both your mind and body.

Recognizing Your Own Stress Triggers

Understanding the root causes of your financial stress is essential for managing and overcoming it. Often, financial stress doesn't stem from just one source, but rather a combination of factors. By identifying your specific triggers, you can take targeted steps to reduce your anxiety and develop a plan that suits your situation. Recognizing your own stress triggers requires honest reflection on your habits, emotions, and the circumstances surrounding your finances.

One of the most common financial stress triggers is uncertainty about income. This could be due to fluctuating pay, an unstable job market, or the fear of losing a current job. The unpredictable nature of freelance work or self-employment can also contribute to this anxiety. If you're constantly unsure when or how much money will come in, it's natural to feel anxious about how to meet your financial obligations. Understanding that this unpredictability is a significant source of stress for you can help you develop strategies to stabilize your income or create a financial buffer to lessen the worry.

Debt is another major trigger. The pressure of owing money, especially with high-interest rates or mounting credit card balances, can cause significant stress. Seeing bills pile up or watching interest grow faster than you can pay it off can feel overwhelming. The mental burden of being in debt, especially when you're unsure how to manage or reduce it, can create a constant source of anxiety. If you find yourself dreading the arrival of bills or avoiding looking at your credit statements, debt is likely a primary stress trigger.

For some, high living expenses are a key contributor to financial stress. Housing costs, utilities, food, healthcare, and transportation can add up quickly, particularly if they consume a large portion of your income. If you feel like you're constantly struggling just to make ends meet, or if your expenses seem to outweigh your income, this imbalance can cause a constant feeling of being behind financially. You might notice that your stress levels spike whenever you think about rent or when an unexpected expense, like a car repair or medical bill, throws off your budget.

Unexpected costs are a trigger for many people, especially those without an emergency fund or financial safety net. Life is full of surprises—car breakdowns, medical emergencies, home repairs—that can derail your financial plans in an instant. Even when things seem to be going smoothly, the looming fear of an unexpected expense can keep you on edge. Recognizing that this fear is a major source of stress may motivate you to create a small emergency fund, even if it starts with just a few dollars.

Another key trigger for financial stress is a lack of financial knowledge or planning. If you're not sure how to budget, invest, or save, it can be easy to feel out of control when it comes to your finances. You might worry that you're not managing your money properly, which can lead to feelings of helplessness. Similarly, if you're not sure how to plan for the future—whether it's retirement, buying a home, or saving for a big life event—this uncertainty can exacerbate financial stress.

Once you begin to recognize your own triggers, it becomes easier to address them. Reflecting on the areas of your finances that cause the most anxiety will help you take steps toward managing that stress. Whether it's creating a budget, seeking financial advice, or building an emergency fund, identifying the root cause of your anxiety is the first step toward making positive changes. By doing this, you can start to regain control over your financial situation and reduce the mental and emotional toll it takes on you.

CHAPTER 2: ORGANIZING YOUR FINANCES

Creating A Clear Financial Snapshot

Before you can make any meaningful progress toward relieving financial stress, it's essential to understand your current financial situation. Creating a clear financial snapshot gives you a complete and honest picture of where you stand, which is crucial for making informed decisions. By gathering all the necessary details about your income, expenses, savings, and debts, you'll have the foundation needed to start organizing and managing your finances effectively.

Start by documenting your sources of income. This could include your salary or wages, any side jobs or freelance work, investment returns, government benefits, or any other financial support you receive regularly. Make sure to capture the full scope of your income, both fixed and variable. Knowing exactly how much money is coming in each month will help you better understand what you have available to cover your financial obligations.

Next, take a detailed look at your expenses. Break them down into two categories: fixed and variable. Fixed expenses are those that stay the same each month, such as rent or mortgage payments, car loans, insurance premiums, and utility bills. Variable expenses fluctuate based on usage or spending habits—these might include groceries, dining out, entertainment, and transportation costs. Don't forget to account for any irregular or annual expenses, such as car maintenance or holiday spending. It's easy to overlook these costs, but including them in your financial snapshot will ensure you have a full understanding of your spending patterns.

Once you have a handle on your income and expenses, it's time to assess your savings. Consider any savings accounts, emergency funds, retirement accounts, or investments you've set aside. It's important to know how much money you have saved and what those funds are earmarked for. If you don't have savings yet, don't panic—this exercise is about getting a clear view of where you are today, so you can start building toward a more secure future.

Lastly, it's crucial to list all of your debts. This might include credit card balances, student loans, car loans, personal loans, or medical bills. For each debt, make sure to include the balance owed, interest rates, and minimum monthly payments. Understanding how much you owe—and to whom—will be vital in determining the steps you need to take to pay down debt effectively. If you have any high-interest debts, they should be given priority in your financial planning, as they can quickly grow and compound if left unchecked.

By gathering all of this information—income, expenses, savings, and debts—you'll have a comprehensive snapshot of your financial situation. It may feel overwhelming to see everything laid out, but having a clear view of where you stand is a crucial first step. This financial snapshot will not only help you make better decisions moving forward, but it will also allow you to track your progress as you work toward reducing financial stress. From here, you can begin setting goals and creating strategies to improve your financial health, one step at a time.

Setting Up A Simple Budget

Setting up a simple budget is a key step in taking control of your finances and reducing financial stress. A budget gives you a clear understanding of where your money is going, helping you to prioritize spending and avoid unnecessary expenses. Creating a budget may seem daunting at first, but it doesn't have to be complicated. By breaking it down into manageable steps, you can develop a plan that works for your needs.

The first step in setting up your budget is to distinguish between your essential needs and non-essential wants. Needs are things you must pay for to survive and function, such as housing, utilities, groceries, transportation, and healthcare. Wants are the things that add comfort or pleasure to your life but aren't necessary, such as dining out, entertainment, or shopping for clothes beyond what you truly need. When you've clearly defined your needs and wants, you'll be in a better position to assess where your money is going and make adjustments where necessary.

Once you've categorized your expenses, start by allocating your income toward your essential needs. The goal is to make sure that the money you're earning covers these basic expenses first. If you find that your income doesn't fully cover your needs, you may need to adjust your spending, explore ways to increase your income, or look for areas where you can cut costs. On the other hand, if your needs are comfortably covered, you can begin allocating a portion of your income toward your non-essential wants. However, even if you have enough income to cover both needs and wants, it's important to practice mindful spending and ensure that your wants don't take away from your ability to save for the future or manage debt.

Once you've identified where your money should go, create a plan for how much you will allocate to each expense category every month. Be realistic in your approach. If you know you typically spend more in a certain area, like groceries or transportation, make sure your budget reflects that so you don't set yourself up for failure. At the same time, challenge yourself to find areas where you can cut back on non-essential spending. Small adjustments can make a big difference in freeing up funds for savings, debt reduction, or unexpected expenses.

A simple rule to follow when budgeting is the 50/30/20 rule. This guideline suggests that 50% of your income should go toward needs, 30% toward wants, and 20% toward savings or paying down debt. While this rule isn't set in stone, it can provide a helpful framework to ensure that you are covering your basic needs, allowing room for enjoyment, and still making progress toward financial stability.

Finally, it's important to track your spending regularly. Your budget is a living document, not a one-time exercise. By regularly reviewing and adjusting your budget based on your spending habits, you'll stay on track and make sure you're meeting your financial goals. Whether you use a budgeting app, a spreadsheet, or a simple notebook, find a system that works for you and stick to it.

Setting up a simple budget will help you regain control of your finances, reduce stress, and set you on the path toward financial security. It's about being intentional with your money and making sure your spending aligns with your priorities and goals.

Tracking Expenses & Prioritizing Bills

Tracking expenses and prioritizing bills are crucial steps in managing your finances effectively and alleviating financial stress. By keeping a close eye on where your money goes and making sure your bills are paid in a timely manner, you can avoid overspending, manage debt, and ensure that your financial obligations are met.

To start tracking your expenses, begin by recording every purchase or transaction you make. This can be done manually with a notebook or spreadsheet, or through digital tools like budgeting apps or bank statements. The key is to be consistent and detailed, noting the date, amount, and category of each expense. Categories might include groceries, utilities, entertainment, transportation, and more. By keeping track of these expenses, you can gain a clear picture of your spending habits and identify areas where you may be overspending or where adjustments can be made.

Once you have a record of your expenses, analyze them to understand your spending patterns. Compare your actual spending against your budget to see if you are staying within your allocated limits. If you find that you are consistently exceeding your budget in certain areas, consider making adjustments to your spending or revising your budget to better align with your financial reality. Identifying trends and areas for improvement will help you make informed decisions about where to cut back and how to manage your money more effectively.

Prioritizing bills is another essential aspect of managing your finances. Start by listing all of your regular bills, such as rent or mortgage, utilities, credit card payments, and loans. Rank these bills in order of importance, focusing on those that have the most immediate consequences if not paid. For example, housing and utilities are typically high-priority expenses, as failing to pay them can result in serious consequences such as eviction or service interruptions. On the other hand, non-essential expenses, such as subscriptions or discretionary spending, can be adjusted or deferred if necessary.

To ensure that you are meeting your financial obligations, create a payment schedule for your bills. This can be a simple calendar or reminder system that helps you keep track of due dates and amounts owed. Consider setting up automatic payments for recurring bills to avoid missing deadlines and incurring late fees. If automatic payments are not feasible, make it a habit to review your bills and payment deadlines regularly to ensure timely payment.

In addition to managing your regular bills, it is important to build an emergency fund to cover unexpected expenses. Having a financial cushion can prevent you from falling behind on bills and help you avoid accumulating debt in the face of unforeseen circumstances. Aim to set aside a portion of your income each month into an emergency savings account, and use this fund only for genuine emergencies.

By diligently tracking your expenses and prioritizing your bills, you will be better equipped to manage your finances, reduce stress, and work toward your financial goals. Effective expense tracking and bill prioritization not only help you stay on top of your financial commitments but also empower you to make informed decisions about your spending and savings.

CHAPTER 3: REDUCING EXPENSES

Cutting Unnecessary Costs

Reducing unnecessary costs is a vital part of managing your finances and relieving financial stress. By examining your spending habits and identifying areas where you can cut back, you can free up funds and improve your financial situation. Here are some strategies to help you reduce costs in key areas such as utilities, entertainment, and subscriptions.

Start by evaluating your utility bills. There are often simple changes you can make to lower your monthly expenses. For example, adjust your thermostat settings to reduce heating and cooling costs. In the winter, lower the thermostat when you are away from home or while sleeping. In the summer, consider using fans to circulate air and reduce the need for air conditioning. Additionally, unplug electronic devices and chargers when they are not in use, as they continue to draw power even when turned off. Switching to energy-efficient light bulbs and appliances can also lead to significant savings over time.

Entertainment expenses can also add up quickly. Look for ways to enjoy leisure activities without overspending. Take advantage of free or low-cost community events, such as local festivals, concerts, or outdoor activities. Instead of dining out frequently, consider hosting potlucks or game nights at home with friends and family. Exploring free or low-cost entertainment options, such as library programs, hiking, or visiting local parks, can help you enjoy your leisure time without straining your budget.

Subscriptions and memberships are another area where you can often find savings. Review all your subscription services, such as streaming platforms, magazines, or gym memberships. Determine which services you use regularly and which ones you could live without. Cancel or pause subscriptions that you no longer find valuable or that you use infrequently. Many subscription services offer flexible plans, so consider downgrading to a lower tier if you do not need all the features.

In addition to these specific areas, regularly reviewing your overall spending and creating a budget can help you identify other unnecessary costs. Look for patterns in your spending and consider areas where you might be able to cut back. For example, if you frequently purchase coffee or snacks from convenience stores, consider making these items at home instead. Small changes can add up to significant savings over time.

Cutting unnecessary costs is not about depriving yourself but rather about making mindful choices that align with your financial goals. By taking the time to assess your spending habits and making adjustments where needed, you can reduce financial stress and improve your overall financial health.

Frugal Living Tips

Embracing a frugal lifestyle can help you manage your finances more effectively without sacrificing your quality of life. Frugal living is about making thoughtful choices and prioritizing your spending to ensure that every dollar contributes to your financial well-being. Here are some practical tips for incorporating frugality into your daily life:

1. Budget Mindfully: Start by creating a budget that outlines your income, expenses, and financial goals. This will help you

understand where your money is going and where you can make adjustments. Stick to your budget by tracking your expenses and avoiding impulse purchases.

2. Shop Smart: Look for deals, discounts, and coupons when shopping for groceries, clothing, and other necessities. Consider buying in bulk for items you use regularly, which can often reduce the cost per unit. Be mindful of sales and take advantage of them, but only for items you genuinely need.

3. Embrace DIY: Many everyday tasks can be done yourself rather than paying for services. Learn basic skills like cooking, home repairs, or car maintenance. YouTube and online tutorials can provide step-by-step guidance for a variety of DIY projects.

4. Reduce Energy Consumption: Save on utility bills by being more energy-efficient. Turn off lights and unplug appliances when not in use. Use energy-efficient bulbs and consider programmable thermostats to regulate heating and cooling. Small changes in your energy habits can lead to substantial savings.

5. Cut Back on Dining Out: Eating out can be expensive, so reduce how often you dine at restaurants. Plan and prepare meals at home, which is often more cost-effective and healthier. Meal prepping and cooking in bulk can save both time and money.

6. Seek Free Entertainment: There are many enjoyable activities that cost nothing or very little. Explore local parks, attend free community events, or take advantage of library programs. Look for low-cost hobbies and activities that bring you joy without breaking the bank.

7. Make the Most of Your Possessions: Before making new purchases, consider whether you can repurpose or repair existing items. Maintain and take care of your belongings to extend their lifespan. This approach reduces the need for frequent replacements and can save you money.

8. Use Public Transportation: If possible, use public

transportation instead of owning a car or relying on taxis. Public transit can be more affordable and reduce expenses related to car maintenance, insurance, and fuel.

9. Negotiate and Compare Prices: Don't be afraid to negotiate prices on services or large purchases. Compare prices from different providers to ensure you're getting the best deal. This applies to everything from insurance policies to cable services.

10. Focus on Value, Not Status: Avoid spending money on items or experiences just to keep up with others. Instead, focus on spending that aligns with your values and financial goals. Choose value over status to maintain a more sustainable and stress-free lifestyle.

By integrating these frugal living tips into your daily routine, you can achieve financial stability and reduce stress while still enjoying a fulfilling life. Frugality is about making intentional choices and finding satisfaction in simple, cost-effective solutions.

Meal Planning And Shopping Smart

Effective meal planning and smart shopping can significantly reduce your grocery expenses while ensuring you maintain a balanced diet. By implementing these strategies, you can save money and minimize food waste, all while enjoying delicious and nutritious meals.

Start by creating a meal plan for the week. This involves deciding what meals you'll prepare each day, including breakfast, lunch, dinner, and snacks. Planning your meals in advance helps you make a precise shopping list, reducing the likelihood of impulse buys and ensuring you have everything you need. Include recipes that utilize similar ingredients to avoid buying items that may go to waste.

Once you have your meal plan, create a detailed shopping list. List the specific items you need, categorized by sections of the store such as produce, dairy, and grains. Sticking to your list helps prevent unplanned purchases and ensures you don't forget essential ingredients. Check your pantry and refrigerator before shopping to see what items you already have and adjust your list accordingly.

When shopping, consider buying in bulk for non-perishable items or items you use frequently. Bulk buying can lower the cost per unit, but make sure you can use the products before they expire. Focus on purchasing seasonal fruits and vegetables, which are often cheaper and fresher than out-of-season produce.

Take advantage of store promotions, such as discounts and coupons, but only for items you need. Be cautious not to buy items just because they're on sale if they don't fit into your meal plan or are not essential. Also, explore generic or store brands, which can offer similar quality to name brands at a lower price.

Shopping with a list and avoiding unnecessary purchases is crucial, but it's also important to choose the right store. Compare prices across different grocery stores to find the best deals. Some stores may offer lower prices on specific items, so shopping at multiple locations for the best prices can be worthwhile if it saves you money.

Additionally, consider preparing meals in advance or cooking in batches. Batch cooking involves making larger quantities of food that can be portioned out and frozen for later use. This not only saves time but also reduces the temptation to dine out or order takeout.

Lastly, practice portion control and store leftovers properly. Use airtight containers to keep leftovers fresh and ensure that you use them within a few days. Properly stored leftovers can be used for future meals, reducing food waste and further stretching your grocery budget.

By adopting these meal planning and shopping smart strategies, you can efficiently manage your grocery expenses, reduce food waste, and enjoy a variety of nutritious meals. This approach not only helps you save money but also contributes to a more organized and stress-free kitchen routine.

CHAPTER 4: BUILDING FINANCIAL RESILIENCE

Creating An Emergency Fund

An emergency fund is a crucial component of financial resilience, providing a safety net for unexpected expenses such as medical emergencies, car repairs, or job loss. Establishing this fund ensures that you are prepared for life's unforeseen events and can help reduce the financial stress associated with emergencies.

To start building an emergency fund, first determine how much you need. A common recommendation is to save three to six months' worth of living expenses. This amount can vary based on your personal circumstances and comfort level. If saving this amount seems daunting, begin with a smaller, manageable goal, such as $500 or $1,000. As you build your savings, you can gradually increase this amount.

Begin by assessing your current financial situation and identifying areas where you can cut back to allocate funds for your emergency savings. Review your budget to find discretionary spending that can be reduced or eliminated. This might include dining out less frequently, canceling unused subscriptions, or scaling back on non-essential purchases.

Next, set up a dedicated savings account for your emergency fund. Choose a high-yield savings account or money market account to maximize your interest earnings while keeping your funds easily accessible. Avoid keeping your emergency fund in your primary checking account, as it can be tempting to dip into it for non-emergencies.

Automate your savings to ensure consistency. Set up automatic transfers from your checking account to your emergency fund on a regular basis, such as bi-weekly or monthly. Treat these transfers as a fixed expense, prioritizing them just like you would with rent or utilities. Even small, regular contributions can add up over time.

If you're on a tight budget, finding ways to save for your emergency fund can be challenging but not impossible. Consider setting aside any extra income, such as tax refunds, bonuses, or cash gifts. Additionally, find opportunities to save on everyday expenses. Use coupons, take advantage of sales, and look for discounts to free up additional funds for your savings.

It's also helpful to regularly review and adjust your savings goals as your financial situation changes. If you receive a raise or reduce debt, redirect some of those funds toward increasing your emergency fund. Likewise, if you encounter unexpected expenses or changes in income, reassess your savings plan to stay on track.

Building an emergency fund requires patience and discipline, but the peace of mind it provides is invaluable. By starting with manageable goals, automating your savings, and making incremental adjustments, you can establish a financial cushion that protects you from life's uncertainties and contributes to long-term financial stability.

Finding Ways To Increase Income

Increasing your income can be an effective strategy for improving your financial situation and building resilience against unexpected expenses. By diversifying your sources of income, you not only enhance your financial stability but also gain more flexibility in managing your budget and achieving your financial goals. Here are several approaches to consider for boosting your income:

Explore Side Gigs: Side gigs offer a flexible way to earn extra money without committing to a full-time job. Depending on your skills and interests, options may include driving for a ride-sharing service, delivering food, pet sitting, or freelancing in areas like writing, graphic design, or web development. Look for opportunities that align with your strengths and schedule, and evaluate which side gigs fit best with your current lifestyle.

Freelance Work: Freelancing allows you to leverage your professional skills on a project-by-project basis. Websites like Upwork, Freelancer, and Fiverr provide platforms where you can offer services in various fields such as writing, marketing, consulting, and more. Building a strong profile and portfolio can help attract clients and establish a steady stream of freelance work.

Sell Unused Items: Decluttering your home and selling items you no longer need can be a practical way to generate extra cash. Consider selling clothing, electronics, furniture, or collectibles through online marketplaces like eBay, Craigslist, or Facebook Marketplace. Organize a garage sale or participate in local swap meets to reach buyers in your community.

Monetize Hobbies and Skills: Turn your passions into income by offering services or products related to your hobbies. For example, if you enjoy crafting, you could sell handmade goods on Etsy. If you're a skilled photographer, offer portrait sessions or event photography. Monetizing your hobbies not only boosts your income but also provides a fulfilling way to engage with what you love.

Part-Time Jobs: If your schedule allows, taking on a part-time job can provide a steady source of additional income. Look for positions that complement your main job or offer flexible hours.

Retail, hospitality, and customer service sectors often have part-time openings that can fit around your existing commitments.

Rent Out Property or Space: If you have extra space in your home or property, consider renting it out to generate passive income. Options include renting a spare room on platforms like Airbnb, leasing a parking space, or renting out storage space. Ensure that you comply with local regulations and understand the responsibilities of being a landlord.

Invest in Your Education: Investing in courses or certifications can open doors to higher-paying job opportunities or career advancement. Research industry trends to identify skills in demand and pursue relevant education or training. This long-term strategy can lead to increased earning potential and career growth.

Explore Online Opportunities: The digital landscape offers numerous ways to earn money. Consider creating a blog, starting a YouTube channel, or participating in affiliate marketing. Online surveys, market research, and remote customer service positions are also viable options. Be cautious of scams and thoroughly research opportunities before committing.

Increasing your income involves exploring various avenues and leveraging your skills and resources effectively. Whether through side gigs, freelance work, selling unused items, or other methods, finding ways to boost your earnings can significantly enhance your financial well-being and provide greater flexibility in managing your finances.

Understanding and Improving Your Credit Score

Your credit score plays a crucial role in your financial health, influencing everything from loan approval to the interest rates you receive. Understanding how your credit score works and taking steps to improve it can help you achieve better financial opportunities and manage your finances more effectively.

Understanding Your Credit Score

A credit score is a numerical representation of your creditworthiness, calculated based on your credit history. It typically ranges from 300 to 850, with higher scores indicating better creditworthiness. Credit scoring models, such as FICO and VantageScore, consider several factors when calculating your score:

1. Payment History (35%): Your track record of making payments on time is the most significant factor. Late payments, collections, and bankruptcies can negatively impact your score.

2. Credit Utilization (30%): This is the ratio of your current credit card balances to your credit limits. A lower ratio indicates that you're using a smaller portion of your available credit, which is favorable for your score.

3. Length of Credit History (15%): The age of your credit accounts impacts your score. A longer credit history demonstrates your ability to manage credit over time.

4. Types of Credit Accounts (10%): Having a mix of credit types, such as credit cards, installment loans, and retail accounts, can positively influence your score.

5. Recent Credit Inquiries (10%): When you apply for new credit, a hard inquiry is made, which can temporarily lower your score. Frequent applications for new credit can have a negative impact.

Improving Your Credit Score

Improving your credit score requires consistent effort and good financial habits. Here are some practical steps to help you enhance your credit profile:

1. Pay Your Bills on Time: Consistently making on-time payments is essential for maintaining a positive payment history. Set up reminders or automate payments to ensure you never miss a due date.

2. Reduce Credit Card Balances: Aim to lower your credit card balances to reduce your credit utilization ratio. Pay off high-interest debt first and consider using a budget to manage your spending and pay down balances.

3. Avoid Opening Too Many New Accounts: While having a diverse credit mix can be beneficial, opening too many new credit accounts in a short period can negatively affect your score. Only apply for new credit when necessary.

4. Check Your Credit Reports Regularly: Obtain and review your credit reports from the three major credit bureaus—Equifax, Experian, and TransUnion. Look for errors or inaccuracies and dispute any discrepancies with the respective bureau to ensure your report reflects accurate information.

5. Maintain a Healthy Credit Mix: Having a mix of credit types, such as revolving credit cards and installment loans, can positively impact your score. However, only take on credit accounts that you can manage responsibly.

6. Keep Old Accounts Open: The length of your credit history is important, so keep older accounts open even if you're not using them regularly. Closing old accounts can shorten your credit history and potentially lower your score.

7. Manage Your Debt Wisely: Avoid taking on more debt than you can handle. Create a debt repayment plan and focus on reducing existing debt to improve your credit profile over time.

8. Seek Professional Advice if Needed: If you're struggling with debt or managing your credit, consider seeking advice from a financial counselor or credit repair specialist. They can provide

guidance and strategies to help you improve your credit score.

Improving your credit score is a gradual process that requires dedication and responsible financial behavior. By understanding the factors that influence your credit score and taking proactive steps to manage your credit effectively, you can enhance your financial health and open the door to better financial opportunities.

CHAPTER 5: MANAGING DEBT WITHOUT PANIC

Assessing Your Debt

The first step in managing debt is to gain a clear understanding of what you owe. This involves not only tallying up the total amount of debt but also analyzing the specifics of each debt to effectively create a strategy for repayment.

Understanding What You Owe

Start by compiling a comprehensive list of all your debts. This should include credit cards, personal loans, student loans, mortgages, car loans, and any other outstanding obligations. For each debt, note down the following details:

1. Total Amount Owed: The full amount of the principal balance that remains to be repaid.

2. Interest Rates: The annual percentage rate (APR) associated with each debt. Higher interest rates can significantly increase the total cost of borrowing over time.

3. Minimum Payments: The minimum amount required to be paid each month. This is often set by the lender and may vary from one debt to another.

4. Due Dates: The dates when payments are due each month. Keeping track of these dates helps avoid late fees and potential damage to your credit score.

Creating a Debt Profile

With this information, you can create a debt profile or summary that provides a snapshot of your financial obligations. This profile should include a clear breakdown of each debt, organized in a way that highlights the total amount owed, interest rates, and due dates. This overview is crucial for developing a targeted plan to manage and reduce your debt.

Assessing Your Financial Situation

Next, assess your overall financial situation to determine how much you can realistically allocate towards debt repayment. This involves reviewing your income, expenses, and any available assets. Creating a budget that includes a dedicated debt repayment category will help you identify how much extra money you can put towards reducing your debt each month.

Evaluating Debt Types

Different types of debt have varying impacts on your finances and may require different approaches for repayment. For instance, high-interest credit card debt may be more urgent to address compared to lower-interest student loans. By categorizing your debt based on interest rates and amounts, you can prioritize which debts to focus on first.

Considering the Total Debt Picture

Finally, consider how the total amount of debt fits into your overall financial goals and lifestyle. Understanding the full scope of your debt helps in making informed decisions about repayment strategies and financial adjustments. It also provides perspective on the steps needed to regain control of your finances.

Assessing your debt thoroughly is the foundation for effective debt management. By understanding the specifics of what you owe and how it impacts your financial health, you can develop a strategic approach to reduce your debt and work towards a more secure financial future.

Strategies For Paying Off Debt

Once you have a clear understanding of your debt, the next crucial step is to develop a strategy for paying it off effectively. Two popular methods for tackling debt are the snowball method and the avalanche method. Each approach has its own advantages, and the choice depends on your personal preferences and financial situation.

The Snowball Method

The snowball method involves paying off your debts from the smallest balance to the largest. Here's how it works:

1. List Your Debts: Arrange your debts in order from the smallest balance to the largest.

2. Make Minimum Payments: Continue to make the minimum payments on all your debts except for the one with the smallest balance.

3. Focus Extra Funds: Allocate any extra money towards paying off the smallest debt.

4. Celebrate Small Wins: Once the smallest debt is paid off, move to the next smallest debt and repeat the process.

The snowball method is effective because it provides psychological motivation. By achieving quick wins with smaller debts, you gain momentum and confidence, which can help you stay committed to your debt repayment journey.

The Avalanche Method

The avalanche method, on the other hand, focuses on paying off debts with the highest interest rates first. Here's how it works:

1. List Your Debts: Arrange your debts in order from the highest interest rate to the lowest.

2. Make Minimum Payments: Continue to make the minimum payments on all your debts except for the one with the highest interest rate.

3. Focus Extra Funds: Allocate any extra money towards paying off the debt with the highest interest rate.

4. Move to Next Debt: Once the highest interest debt is paid off, apply the extra funds to the next highest interest debt and continue the process.

The avalanche method is generally more cost-effective in the long run because it minimizes the total interest paid over time. It's ideal if your primary goal is to reduce the amount of interest you'll pay on your debt.

Choosing the Right Approach

The decision between the snowball and avalanche methods depends on what motivates you more: seeing quick results or saving on interest. If you're driven by immediate gratification, the snowball method might be more effective. If you're more focused on saving money over time, the avalanche method may be better.

Additional Strategies

1. Debt Consolidation: Consider consolidating multiple debts into a single loan with a lower interest rate. This can simplify payments and potentially reduce interest costs.

2. Negotiate Lower Rates: Reach out to creditors to negotiate lower interest rates on your existing debt. Sometimes, lenders

are willing to accommodate requests if you have a good payment history.

3. Automate Payments: Set up automatic payments to ensure you never miss a due date, which can help avoid late fees and potential credit score damage.

4. Increase Income: Look for opportunities to increase your income through side gigs or additional work. Any extra money earned can be directed towards debt repayment.

By choosing a debt repayment strategy that aligns with your financial situation and goals, you can systematically reduce your debt and work towards achieving financial stability. Remember, consistency and commitment are key to successfully managing and eliminating debt.

Communicating With Creditors

Effective communication with creditors is a critical component of managing and reducing debt. When facing financial challenges, reaching out to creditors can help you negotiate better terms and avoid further complications. Here's how to approach communicating with your creditors to achieve favorable outcomes:

1. Assess Your Situation

Before contacting creditors, evaluate your financial situation comprehensively. Understand your current income, expenses, and the total amount of debt you owe. Be prepared to provide details about your financial situation when you reach out to creditors.

2. Prepare Your Request

Determine what you need from your creditors. Common requests include:

- Lowering Interest Rates: Ask if they can reduce the interest rate on your debt to lower your monthly payments and overall interest costs.

- Payment Plans: Request a more manageable payment plan if you're struggling to meet the current terms.

- Temporary Hardship Relief: Inquire about temporary relief options, such as payment deferrals or forbearance, if you're facing a short-term financial hardship.

3. Contact Your Creditors

Reach out to your creditors through their customer service channels. This can be done via phone, email, or written correspondence. When communicating, be clear and concise about your request. Here's a step-by-step guide:

- Be Honest and Transparent: Explain your financial difficulties honestly and provide evidence if necessary, such as a budget or proof of income reduction.

- Be Polite and Professional: Maintain a polite and professional tone throughout the conversation. Creditor representatives are more likely to assist you if you approach them respectfully.

- Ask About Options: Inquire about available options for adjusting your payment terms or reducing your debt. Ensure you fully understand any terms or conditions associated with these options.

4. Document Everything

Keep detailed records of all communications with your creditors. This includes dates, times, the names of representatives you spoke with, and summaries of the conversations. Written documentation helps protect you and ensures that you have a reference in case of disputes or misunderstandings.

5. Follow Up

After reaching an agreement with a creditor, confirm the terms in writing. Ensure you receive a formal confirmation of any changes made to your account, such as revised payment plans or reduced interest rates. Follow up to verify that the agreed-upon changes have been implemented correctly.

6. Consider Debt Consolidation

If managing multiple debts is overwhelming, explore debt consolidation options. Debt consolidation involves combining several debts into a single loan, often with a lower interest rate. This can simplify your payments and potentially reduce your overall interest costs. Contact lenders or financial institutions to discuss consolidation options and determine if this approach suits your needs.

7. Seek Professional Help

If you find it challenging to negotiate with creditors on your own, consider seeking help from a credit counselor or financial advisor. These professionals can provide guidance on managing debt and negotiating with creditors on your behalf.

Effective communication with creditors can lead to more manageable debt repayment terms and provide relief during financial difficulties. By approaching creditors with a clear plan and maintaining open, honest dialogue, you can work towards improving your financial situation and achieving greater stability.

CHAPTER 6: COPING WITH FINANCIAL ANXIETY

Mindfulness And Stress Reduction

In the face of financial challenges, cultivating mindfulness and stress reduction techniques can play a crucial role in maintaining emotional well-being and making clearer, more rational decisions. Financial stress often impacts both mental and physical health, making it essential to adopt practices that promote relaxation and resilience. Here's how mindfulness and stress reduction can help and how you can incorporate them into your daily routine:

1. Understanding Mindfulness

Mindfulness is the practice of being fully present and engaged in the current moment, without judgment. By focusing on the here and now, you can reduce anxiety and prevent yourself from becoming overwhelmed by future financial worries. Mindfulness helps you observe your thoughts and feelings without being controlled by them, allowing you to approach your financial situation with a calmer and more balanced mindset.

2. Incorporating Mindfulness Techniques

 - Deep Breathing: Practice deep breathing exercises to calm your mind and body. Spend a few minutes each day taking slow, deep breaths, focusing on the sensation of your breath as it moves in and out. This simple practice can help reduce immediate stress and anxiety.

- Meditation: Regular meditation can enhance your ability to handle stress. Start with a few minutes of guided meditation or mindfulness exercises daily. Apps and online resources can provide structured meditation sessions designed to promote relaxation and mental clarity.

- Mindful Reflection: Set aside time for mindful reflection to evaluate your financial situation calmly. Instead of reacting impulsively to financial stress, use this time to reflect on your goals and develop a thoughtful approach to managing your finances.

3. Stress Reduction Techniques

- Physical Activity: Regular physical exercise is a powerful tool for reducing stress. Activities such as walking, yoga, or swimming can help release endorphins, which act as natural mood enhancers. Incorporate exercise into your routine to improve your overall mental and physical health.

- Healthy Eating: Maintain a balanced diet to support your body's ability to handle stress. Nutrient-rich foods can improve mood and energy levels, helping you stay focused and resilient in the face of financial challenges.

- Adequate Sleep: Ensure you get enough quality sleep each night. Poor sleep can exacerbate stress and impair your decision-making abilities. Establish a consistent sleep schedule and create a restful environment to promote better sleep.

4. Developing Healthy Habits

- Set Realistic Goals: Break down your financial goals into manageable steps. By setting realistic, achievable objectives, you can create a sense of progress and reduce feelings of overwhelm. Celebrate small victories along the way to maintain motivation and confidence.

- Practice Gratitude: Focus on the positive aspects of your life and practice gratitude. Reflect on what you are thankful for each day, which can help shift your perspective away from financial stress and foster a more positive mindset.

5. Seeking Support

- Talk to Someone: Don't hesitate to seek support from friends, family, or a mental health professional. Sharing your concerns with someone you trust can provide emotional relief and offer new perspectives on your financial challenges.

- Join Support Groups: Consider joining support groups or online communities where you can connect with others facing similar financial issues. Sharing experiences and strategies with others can provide valuable insights and encouragement.

Incorporating mindfulness and stress reduction techniques into your routine can significantly impact your ability to manage financial stress effectively. By adopting these practices, you can enhance your resilience, improve your emotional well-being, and approach your financial challenges with a clearer, more balanced perspective.

How To Talk About Money Stress

Addressing financial stress with honesty and openness can be a powerful step toward alleviating its impact and finding support. Talking about money stress is not always easy, but it is crucial for managing your financial well-being and building stronger relationships. Here's how to approach these conversations effectively:

1. Choose the Right Time and Place

- Find a Comfortable Setting: Ensure you are in a comfortable and private environment where you can speak openly without interruptions. This helps create a safe space for discussing sensitive topics.

- Select an Appropriate Time: Choose a time when both you and the other person are calm and able to focus on the conversation. Avoid discussing financial stress during high-stress moments or when emotions are running high.

2. Be Honest and Clear

- Express Your Feelings: Start by expressing your feelings and concerns honestly. Use "I" statements to convey how the financial stress is affecting you personally, such as "I've been feeling overwhelmed by my finances lately" or "I'm struggling to manage my budget and it's causing me a lot of stress."

- Provide Specifics: Share specific details about your financial situation if you feel comfortable doing so. This might include mentioning particular challenges you are facing, such as debt, income instability, or unexpected expenses.

3. Focus on Solutions and Support

- Discuss Potential Solutions: Frame the conversation around finding solutions and seeking support. For example, you might say, "I'm looking for ways to better manage my budget. Do you have any advice or resources that might help?"

- Seek Understanding: Ask for empathy and understanding from the other person. You might say, "I really need someone to listen and understand what I'm going through. Can we talk about this?"

4. Set Boundaries and Respect Privacy

- Be Clear About Boundaries: If there are certain aspects of your financial situation that you prefer not to discuss, set clear boundaries. For example, you can say, "I'm not comfortable sharing the details of my debt, but I appreciate your support."

- Respect Privacy: Similarly, be respectful of others' boundaries and privacy when they are sharing their financial stress. Avoid prying or making judgments, and focus on providing support and understanding.

5. Utilize Support Resources

- Consider Professional Help: If discussing financial stress with friends or family feels difficult, consider seeking support from a financial advisor or counselor. Professionals can offer expert guidance and provide a non-judgmental space to explore your financial concerns.
- Explore Support Groups: Look for support groups or online communities where you can connect with others who are experiencing similar financial challenges. Sharing experiences and advice within these groups can be comforting and helpful.

6. Practice Active Listening

- Listen Attentively: When others are sharing their financial stress with you, practice active listening. Give them your full attention, validate their feelings, and offer supportive feedback.
- Show Empathy: Demonstrate empathy by acknowledging their feelings and offering reassurance. For example, you might say, "I understand how challenging this must be for you. You're not alone in this."

7. Plan Follow-Up Conversations

- Schedule Check-Ins: If the discussion reveals ongoing challenges, plan follow-up conversations to continue offering support and tracking progress. Regular check-ins can help both parties stay engaged and address any new issues that arise.

Talking about money stress openly can foster stronger connections, reduce feelings of isolation, and lead to effective problem-solving. By approaching these conversations with honesty, empathy, and a focus on solutions, you can navigate financial challenges more effectively and build a supportive network.

Building A Support System

Creating a robust support system is essential for managing financial stress effectively and improving your overall well-being. A strong support network provides emotional reassurance, practical advice, and tangible assistance during challenging times. Here's how to build a support system that can help you navigate financial stress:

1. Identify Your Needs

- Assess What Support You Need: Determine what kind of support would be most beneficial for you. This might include emotional support, practical advice, financial guidance, or help with budgeting and debt management.
- Consider Different Types of Support: Recognize that support can come in various forms, including friends, family, professional advisors, and support groups.

2. Reach Out to Friends and Family

- Communicate Openly: Share your financial challenges with trusted friends and family members. Be open about what you're experiencing and let them know how they can support you.
- Seek Emotional Support: Your loved ones can offer emotional reassurance and a listening ear, helping you feel less isolated and more understood.

3. Connect with Financial Professionals

- Consult Financial Advisors: A financial advisor can provide expert guidance on managing your finances, creating a budget, and developing a plan to tackle debt. They can also offer strategies tailored to your specific situation.
- Explore Credit Counselors: Credit counselors specialize in helping individuals manage and reduce debt. They can work with you to create a debt repayment plan and negotiate with creditors.

4. Join Support Groups

- Find Relevant Groups: Look for local or online support groups that focus on financial stress or specific issues you're facing, such as debt management or budgeting. Connecting with others who have similar experiences can provide valuable insights and encouragement.
- Participate Actively: Engage in group discussions, share your experiences, and offer support to others. Active participation can help you build meaningful connections and gain new perspectives.

5. Utilize Online Resources

- Explore Online Forums and Communities: There are many online platforms where you can find communities focused on financial health and stress management. These forums often provide advice, support, and resources that can be helpful.
- Follow Educational Content: Seek out blogs, podcasts, and social media accounts that offer financial advice and stress management tips. Engaging with this content can provide valuable knowledge and support.

6. Build Relationships with Mentors

- Find a Mentor: Consider finding a mentor who has experience in managing finances and overcoming financial challenges. A mentor can offer practical advice, share their experiences, and provide encouragement.
- Establish Regular Check-Ins: Schedule regular meetings or check-ins with your mentor to discuss your progress and any new challenges that arise.

7. Engage in Community Resources

- Look for Local Organizations: Many communities offer resources and programs designed to help individuals manage financial stress. These might include workshops, financial education classes, and counseling services.

- Utilize Non-Profit Services: Non-profit organizations often provide free or low-cost financial counseling, budgeting assistance, and support for those in financial distress.

8. Foster a Supportive Environment

- Create a Positive Atmosphere: Surround yourself with people who are positive and supportive. A nurturing environment can help you stay motivated and focused on your financial goals.

- Encourage Mutual Support: Build reciprocal relationships where both you and your support network members can offer and receive support. Mutual assistance strengthens relationships and provides a sense of community.

Building a support system requires effort and openness, but it is a crucial step in managing financial stress. By seeking out and nurturing relationships with friends, family, professionals, and community resources, you can create a network that offers both practical help and emotional comfort during challenging times.

CHAPTER 7: PLANNING FOR THE FUTURE

Setting Financial Goals

Establishing clear, actionable financial goals is essential for creating a stable and secure financial future. Goals provide direction, motivation, and a framework for managing your money effectively. Here's how to set achievable short-term and long-term financial goals:

1. Define Your Goals Clearly

   - Short-Term Goals: These are objectives you aim to achieve within the next year. Examples include paying off a credit card, saving for a vacation, or building an emergency fund. Short-term goals should be specific, measurable, and attainable within a short time frame.
   - Long-Term Goals: These are aspirations you plan to reach in several years or more. They might include buying a home, funding your children's education, or planning for retirement. Long-term goals require more planning and resources but provide a vision for your financial future.

2. Make Your Goals SMART

   - Specific: Clearly define what you want to achieve. Instead of saying "save money," specify "save $500 for a vacation."
   - Measurable: Determine how you will track your progress. For example, if your goal is to save $500, plan how you will measure

the savings as you go.

- Achievable: Set goals that are realistic based on your current financial situation. Ensure you have the means to achieve them within the given timeframe.

- Relevant: Your goals should align with your overall financial situation and priorities. Ensure that they reflect what is most important to you.

- Time-Bound: Establish a deadline for achieving each goal. A specific time frame helps maintain focus and motivation.

3. Break Down Goals into Manageable Steps

- Create Action Plans: Divide larger goals into smaller, manageable tasks. For example, if you want to save $1,000 in six months, break it down into saving approximately $167 per month.

- Set Milestones: Identify key milestones that mark progress toward your larger goals. Celebrating these smaller achievements can keep you motivated.

4. Prioritize Your Goals

- Evaluate Importance: Determine which goals are most crucial based on your financial situation and personal priorities. Prioritize goals that will have the most significant impact on your well-being and financial stability.

- Allocate Resources: Decide how to allocate your income and savings to meet your prioritized goals. This might involve adjusting your budget or cutting back on non-essential expenses.

5. Monitor and Adjust Your Goals

- Track Progress: Regularly review your progress toward each goal. Use budgeting tools or financial apps to keep track of your savings and spending.

- Adjust as Needed: Be flexible and willing to adjust your goals if your financial situation changes. Revisiting and revising your goals ensures they remain relevant and achievable.

6. Seek Accountability and Support

- Share Your Goals: Discuss your financial goals with a trusted friend or family member. Sharing your goals can provide accountability and encouragement.
- Consider Professional Guidance: If needed, consult a financial advisor to help you set realistic goals and develop a plan to achieve them.

By setting clear, actionable financial goals, you create a roadmap for managing your money and achieving financial stability. Whether you're focusing on short-term objectives or planning for long-term aspirations, a well-defined goal-setting strategy helps guide your financial decisions and keeps you motivated as you work toward a secure and prosperous future.

Creating A Realistic Savings Plan

A well-crafted savings plan is crucial for achieving financial stability and reaching your financial goals. Whether you're saving for an emergency fund, a major purchase, or future investments, a realistic and structured approach to saving helps ensure success. Here's how to create a savings plan that fits your financial situation and goals:

1. Set Clear Savings Goals

- Define Your Objectives: Start by identifying what you are saving for. This could include an emergency fund, a vacation, a new car, or retirement. Clear goals give you a sense of purpose and direction for your savings efforts.
- Determine the Amount Needed: Calculate how much money you need to achieve each goal. This involves estimating the total cost and setting a target amount to save.

2. Create a Budget

- Track Your Income and Expenses: Develop a budget that outlines your monthly income and expenses. Understanding where your money goes each month helps you identify how much you can realistically set aside for savings.

- Allocate Funds for Savings: Include a specific amount or percentage of your income to be dedicated to savings. Treat savings as a fixed expense, similar to paying bills, to ensure consistency.

3. Choose a Savings Method

- Traditional Savings Account: For short-term goals or an emergency fund, a high-yield savings account offers liquidity and a modest interest rate.

- Certificates of Deposit (CDs): For medium-term goals, CDs offer higher interest rates but require you to lock in your money for a specified period.

- Retirement Accounts: For long-term goals, such as retirement, consider contributing to retirement accounts like a 401(k) or IRA, which offer tax benefits.

4. Automate Your Savings

- Set Up Automatic Transfers: Automate your savings by setting up regular transfers from your checking account to your savings account. This reduces the temptation to spend and ensures consistent contributions.

- Use Direct Deposit: If possible, have a portion of your paycheck directly deposited into your savings account. This makes saving a priority by removing it from your discretionary spending.

5. Adjust Your Savings Plan as Needed

- Review and Adjust: Regularly review your budget and savings plan to ensure it aligns with your financial goals. Adjust the amount you save if your income or expenses change.

- Increase Savings Gradually: As your financial situation improves, consider increasing your savings rate. Small, incremental increases can significantly boost your savings over time.

6. Monitor and Track Your Progress

   - Keep an Eye on Your Goals: Use financial tools or apps to track your savings progress. Monitoring your progress helps you stay motivated and make adjustments if necessary.
   - Celebrate Milestones: Recognize and celebrate when you reach savings milestones. Acknowledging your achievements can keep you motivated and committed to your savings plan.

7. Cut Costs and Boost Savings

   - Identify Areas to Save: Look for areas in your budget where you can cut costs and redirect those savings toward your goals. This might include reducing discretionary spending or finding more affordable alternatives for regular expenses.
   - Take Advantage of Windfalls: Use unexpected financial gains, such as bonuses or tax refunds, to boost your savings. Applying these windfalls directly to your savings goals can accelerate progress.

Creating a realistic savings plan involves setting clear goals, budgeting wisely, choosing appropriate savings methods, and regularly reviewing your progress. By automating your savings, adjusting as needed, and monitoring your efforts, you build a strong foundation for achieving your financial objectives and ensuring long-term financial security.

Investing 101

Investing is a key tool for growing your wealth over time and achieving long-term financial goals, such as retirement or building a financial safety net. While investing may seem intimidating, starting with basic, low-risk strategies can help you feel more comfortable and confident. In this section, we'll introduce some simple concepts to get you started with investing.

1. Why Invest?

Investing allows your money to grow beyond what you could achieve with savings alone. While savings accounts are useful for short-term needs or emergency funds, they typically offer very low returns, especially when adjusted for inflation. In contrast, investing in assets like stocks, bonds, or mutual funds has the potential to generate significantly higher returns over time. By taking a long-term approach to investing, you can grow your wealth steadily and combat the effects of inflation.

2. Understanding Risk vs. Reward

Every investment comes with some level of risk, but understanding how to balance risk and reward is essential to successful investing. Higher-risk investments, like stocks, tend to offer higher potential returns but can fluctuate in value. Lower-risk investments, like bonds or certificates of deposit (CDs), provide more stability but offer lower returns.

- Risk Tolerance: Consider your personal risk tolerance when deciding on investments. If the idea of losing money stresses you out, you may prefer low-risk investments. If you're comfortable with the ups and downs of the market and can invest for the long-term, you might choose to allocate more to higher-risk investments like stocks.

3. Investment Types

- Stocks: When you buy a share of stock, you're purchasing a small ownership stake in a company. Over time, the value of that stock can go up or down based on the company's performance and market conditions. Stocks tend to offer the highest potential for growth but also come with greater risk.

- Bonds: Bonds are essentially loans that you give to a government or corporation in exchange for regular interest payments. They are considered a safer investment compared to stocks because they provide more stable returns. However, the potential for high returns is lower.

- Mutual Funds and ETFs: Mutual funds and Exchange-Traded Funds (ETFs) pool money from many investors to buy a diversified portfolio of stocks, bonds, or other assets. These funds are managed by professionals, making them a good option for beginners who want diversification without picking individual stocks. ETFs trade like stocks on the stock market, while mutual funds are bought directly from the investment company.

- Index Funds: A type of mutual fund or ETF that aims to match the performance of a specific index, like the S&P 500. Index funds are generally low-cost and considered a solid, low-risk investment strategy because they track the overall market rather than trying to beat it.

4. Time in the Market vs. Timing the Market

One of the most important principles in investing is that "time in the market" beats "timing the market." This means that consistently staying invested over the long-term is typically more successful than trying to buy or sell at just the right moment to maximize returns. The stock market fluctuates in the short term, but over longer periods (10+ years), it tends to trend upwards.

5. How to Start Investing

- Start Small: You don't need a large sum of money to begin

investing. Many online brokerages allow you to start with small amounts, and some even offer fractional shares, allowing you to buy a portion of a stock rather than a full share.

- Automate Investments: Many platforms allow you to set up automatic contributions to your investment account. Automating this process helps you stay consistent and makes it easier to grow your portfolio over time.

- Diversify Your Portfolio: Diversification means spreading your investments across different asset classes, such as stocks, bonds, and real estate, to reduce risk. A diversified portfolio ensures that if one type of investment performs poorly, others may still generate positive returns.

6. Retirement Accounts

For many people, retirement accounts are a primary vehicle for investing. Contributions to retirement accounts like 401(k)s, IRAs, or Roth IRAs can provide tax advantages while allowing you to invest in a range of assets. Many employers also offer matching contributions to 401(k) plans, making them a great way to boost your retirement savings.

7. Staying the Course

Investing is a long-term strategy, and it's normal for the value of your investments to fluctuate. During periods of market volatility, it's easy to feel anxious and consider pulling out your money. However, reacting to short-term changes can lead to missing out on long-term gains. Stick to your investment strategy and remember that investing is about building wealth gradually over many years.

Investing doesn't have to be complicated or overwhelming. By starting with small, consistent contributions and focusing on low-risk, diversified options like index funds or ETFs, you can grow your wealth over time. Keep a long-term perspective, avoid trying to time the market, and regularly review your investments to ensure they align with your financial goals.

CONCLUSION

Financial Stress Is Manageable

Throughout this book, we've explored various strategies and techniques to help you navigate and alleviate financial stress. By understanding the root causes of your financial anxiety, you can start to take control of your situation with a clear and organized approach. Creating a comprehensive financial snapshot, setting up a realistic budget, and cutting unnecessary costs are foundational steps in managing your finances effectively.

We have also covered the importance of building an emergency fund and exploring ways to increase your income to enhance your financial resilience. Understanding and improving your credit score further empowers you to make informed financial decisions and secure better terms for loans and credit.

Managing debt without panic involves assessing your liabilities, choosing effective repayment strategies, and communicating with creditors to find manageable solutions. Additionally, incorporating mindfulness and stress reduction techniques can play a crucial role in maintaining your mental well-being during challenging financial times.

Building a support system and learning how to talk openly about money stress can provide the emotional and practical support needed to overcome obstacles. Setting financial goals and creating a realistic savings plan, along with understanding basic investing principles, will guide you towards long-term financial stability and growth.

Where To Go From Here

As you move forward, remember that financial well-being is a journey rather than a destination. The strategies and insights shared in this book are meant to be practical tools that you can adapt to your unique circumstances. Regularly reviewing your financial situation, setting new goals, and adjusting your plans as needed will help you stay on track and continue to build financial security.

Take proactive steps to implement what you've learned, and don't hesitate to seek additional resources or professional advice if needed. Financial stress can feel overwhelming, but with patience, persistence, and the right strategies, you can regain control and create a more secure and peaceful financial future. Remember, the path to financial stability is a process, and each step you take brings you closer to a healthier relationship with your finances.

www.ingramcontent.com/pod-product-compliance
Lightning Source LLC
Chambersburg PA
CBHW051535240526
45471CB00020B/2894